Make a Meal with Marmite

Sweet Savory Recipes – Spread the Word; Love Marmite!

BY

Christina Tosch

Copyright Notes

Table of Contents

Introduction

Marmite is good for you, it's a great source of folic acid and is rich in vitamin-B, but it goes way beyond a spread.

This iconic British food staple is used worldwide to flavor foods and is a versatile sweet and savory recipe ingredient for all kinds of meals.

Here are some more marvelous Marmite facts!

- German scientist, Justus von Liebig, invented Marmite in the late 19th century. It became a spread in the brewing town of Burton, England, in 1902 thanks to the formation of the Marmite Food Company Limited.
- Made from yeast extract, Marmite is a beer-brewing by product.
- The recipe for Marmite remains unchanged throughout its whole history.
- Marmite gets its name from the French earthenware pot or casserole dish, which you can see depicted on British Marmite jars.
- During the First World War, the spread was included in British troop's food rations.
- World Marmite Day falls every year on 28th September.
- Annual sales of Marmite are around 46 million pounds.
- In 1996, advertising agency DDB came up with the popular slogan 'Love it or Hate It'.
- Rumor has it that in 2002 and 2009, UK prisoners were making alcohol using fermented fruit and Marmite.
- On 17th April 2018 Andre Ortolf of Germany ate 368 grams (12.98 ounces) of Marmite in just 60 seconds.
- Dissolve Marmite in boiling water, add fresh lime juice along with a slice of fried onion, and what do you have? A Sri Lankan hangover cure recipe!
- Marmite works equally as well in sweet recipes as it does in savory ones.
- The Rolling Stones, Dido, and Britney Spears love Marmite, but Material Girl, Madonna hates it!

So, say yes to the yeast, spread the love, and make a meal of Marmite with these 40 sweet and savory recipes.

Lite Bites

BBQ Marmite Chicken Wings

Not only is Marmite a sensational spread, but it is also the perfect marinade ingredient for savory foods too.

Servings: 4

Total Time: 8hours 30mins

Ingredients:

- 1 tbsp Marmite
- 1 tbsp soy sauce
- 1 tbsp cracked black pepper
- 1 tbsp rice wine vinegar
- 10 chicken wings (jointed)
- 2 fresh lemons (quartered, to serve)

Directions:

1. Add the Marmite to a large bowl along with the soy sauce, black pepper, and rice wine vinegar. Stir thoroughly to combine.

2. Add the wings to the bowl and coat evenly in the marinade.

3. Cover the bowl and set aside for 6-8 hours to marinate. Shake the bowl every 60 minutes.

4. Preheat your oven to 400 degrees F.

5. In a single layer and not touching one another, place the chicken wings on a baking rack set over a grill pan or baking tray.

6. Cook for 25 minutes or until they reach an internal temperature of 165 degrees F.

7. Serve with quarters of fresh lemon for squeezing.

BBQ Prawn Ciabatta Rolls

Who would ever have thought that this iconic British product would make such a marvelous marinade ingredient for juicy, jumbo prawns?

Servings: 4

Total Time: 35mins

Ingredients:

- ½ cup tomato sauce
- 2 tbsp Marmite
- Tabasco sauce (to taste)
- 16 jumbo green banana prawns (peeled and deveined)
- 1 cup store-bought coleslaw
- 4 ciabatta rolls (split and chargrilled)

Directions:

1. In a bowl, whisk the tomato sauce with the Marmite and Tabasco sauce. Set approximately half of the tomato sauce to one side. Marinate the prawns in the remaining half of the mixture for 7-10 minutes.

2. Remove the prawns from the marinade, shaking off any excess. Discard the marinade.

3. Chargrill the prawns along with the rolls for 2-3 minutes, until they are cooked through.

4. Spoon the store-bought coleslaw onto the bottom half of the rolls, and top with the cooked prawns along with a drizzle of sauce.

5. Enjoy.

Beef Nachos

Marmite will significantly enhance the meat's flavor, making these beef nachos a sensational lite bite to share.

Servings: 4

Total Time: 55mins

Ingredients:

Chili Beef:

- 1 tbsp olive oil
- 1 onion (peeled and finely diced)
- 1 pound lean beef mince
- 1 (14 ounces) can chopped tomatoes
- 1 (14 ounces) can red kidney beans (rinsed and drained)
- 2 tbsp Marmite
- 2 tbsp tomato paste
- Dried red chili flakes (to taste)
- $\frac{1}{3}$ cup water

Guacamole:

- 2 ripe avocados (halved, peeled and pitted)
- 1 tbsp freshly squeezed lemon juice
- 2 ripe tomatoes (finely chopped)
- Salt and black pepper

Nachos:

- 7 ounces corn chips
- 1 cup pizza blend cheese (grated)
- 3 tbsp sour cream
- $\frac{1}{4}$ cup coriander leaves (coarsely chopped)

Directions:

1. In a pan, heat the oil.

2. Add the onion to the pan and sauté until softened, for 5 minutes.

3. Next, add the beef to the pan and cook for 5-8 minutes until browned gently.

4. Add the tomatoes, kidney beans, Marmite, tomato paste, chili flakes, and water. Stir well to combine, and simmer until thickened, for 20-30 minutes.

5. In the meantime, add the avocado to a bowl and with a metal fork mash until smooth. Add the freshly squeezed lemon juice along with the tomato, salt, and black pepper, and stir thoroughly to combine. Put to one side.

6. Preheat your grill to moderate heat.

7. Arrange the corn chips in an ovenproof dish and top with the chili beef.

8. Scatter the cheese over the top and cook until the grill until the cheese melts and is golden, this will take 4-6 minutes.

9. Serve the nachos with guacamole, sour cream, and chopped coriander.

Broccoli and Marmite Soup

This soup is kind on the purse, and a great way to make sure your family gets a healthy portion of fresh veggies.

Servings: 4

Total Time: 45mins

Ingredients:

- Splash of olive oil
- 1 onion (peeled and diced)
- 2 sticks of celery (finely sliced)
- 2 garlic cloves (peeled and minced)
- 1 broccoli head and stalks (chopped into bite-sized pieces)
- 2 small potatoes (peeled and diced)
- Freshly ground black pepper
- 1¼ tsp Marmite
- 2 cups vegetable stock

Directions:

1. Add a splash of oil to a pan and heat.

2. Add the onions to the pan along with the celery and fry for 2-3 minutes before adding the garlic and stirring briskly for an additional 60 seconds.

3. Next, add the broccoli and potatoes and season with fresh black pepper.

4. Stir in the Marmite along with the stock. Bring to boil and turn the heat down. Simmer, covered for approximately 20 minutes. Set aside to cool slightly.

5. Process the soup until smooth in a food blender and reheat.

6. Serve and enjoy.

Cheesy Marmite Loaf

Tear and share this crusty loaf stuffed with Cheddar cheese and Marmite.

Servings: 6-8

Total Time: 20mins

Ingredients:

- 1 crusty sharing bread loaf
- 3 tbsp butter (melted)
- 6 ounces Cheddar cheese (grated)
- 1 tbsp fresh parsley (chopped)
- Marmite (as needed)

Directions:

1. Preheat the main oven to 355 degrees F.

2. Using a sharp knife, make diagonal cuts in the loaf, 1" apart, and making sure you don't slice the bread all the way through.

3. Drizzle the melted butter into the cuts in the bread.

4. Stuff the grated Cheddar cheese and parsley into the cuts and smear Marmite over the top.

5. Using aluminum foil, line a baking tray, and place the loaf on top. Wrap a second sheet of aluminum foil over the top.

6. Bake in the oven for 15 minutes, until the cheese is melted.

7. Remove the aluminum foil form the top and bake in the oven for 12-15 minutes, until the bread is crusty.

8. Serve warm.

English Muffin Marmite Pizza

This pizza-style muffin snack is ready in no time at all. It makes a perfect lite bite for anyone working from home.

Serving: 1-2

Total Time: 5mins

Ingredients:

- 1 English muffin (split in half)
- Butter (to spread)
- Marmite (to taste)
- 2 slices deli salami
- 2 American cheese slices
- 4 medium mushrooms (sliced)
- 1 large tomato (sliced)

Directions:

1. Spread the cut side of the English muffin with butter and Marmite.

2. Layer a slice of salami on each half, followed by a slice of American cheese, sliced mushrooms, and tomatoes.

3. Place the muffins, filled half facing upwards under a hot grill and grill until the cheese is entirely melted.

4. Drizzle with more Marmite and enjoy.

Filo Fingers

Potato, cheese, and Marmite encased in melt-in-the-mouth filo pastry are a tasty lite bite to enjoy on their own or with a mixed salad.

Servings: 10

Total Time: 35mins

Ingredients:

- 2 tbsp oil
- 6 spring onions (peeled and finely chopped)
- 1 pound 5 ounces potatoes (peeled, grated, and drained)
- 2 cloves garlic (peeled and crushed)
- ¼ cup parsley (chopped)
- 1 tbsp Marmite
- Finely grated rind 1 lemon
- 1½ cups Cheddar cheese (grated)
- 10 sheets store-bought filo pastry
- Olive oil nonstick cooking spray
- Tomato chutney (to serve, optional)

Directions:

1. In a frying pan, heat the oil.

2. Add the onions to the pan and cook for 2 minutes.

3. Add the potatoes and garlic and cook gently until fork-tender, for 15 minutes.

4. Stir in the parsley, Marmite, lemon rind, and 1 cup of Cheddar cheese. Put to one side to cool.

5. Fold a sheet of the filo pastry crosswise, in half.

6. Add 2 tablespoons of the filling onto the shortest edge of the filo pastry. Fold the end of the pastry to cover the mixture, fold in the sides and roll to enclose.

7. Spritz with nonstick cooking spray and arrange on a baking tray. Repeat the process with the remaining filo pastry and filling.

8. Scatter the remaining cheese over the filo fingers, and bake in the oven at 390 degrees F, until golden for 15-20 minutes.

9. Serve either cold or warm with a dollop of tomato chutney.

Marmite Sausage Rolls

You and your friends will love these homemade sausage rolls. They are way better than any you can buy and the secret ingredient is, you guessed it; Marmite!

Servings: 16

Total Time: 1hour

Ingredients:

- Knob of butter
- 5¼ ounces chestnut mushrooms (finely chopped)
- 1 tbsp Marmite
- 14 ounces pork sausages (skinned)
- 1 small red onion (peeled and finely chopped)
- 2 tbsp thyme leaves (chopped)
- Salt and black pepper (to season)
- Plain flour (to dust)
- 1 (7½ ounces) sheet frozen store-bought all-butter pastry (thawed)
- 1 egg (beaten)
- 1 tbsp sesame seeds

Directions:

1. In a large frying pan, heat the butter until it foams.

2. Add the mushrooms to the pan and over high heat, cook for 3-5 minutes, until the liquid is evaporated and the mushrooms are browned.

3. Stir in the Marmite and set aside to cool before mixing in the sausage meat, red onion, and chopped thyme leaves. Season with salt and pepper.

4. On a lightly floured, clean work surface, unroll the pastry. Halve the pastry, lengthways and roll each piece out approximately ⅛" wider.

5. Divide the sausage meat into 2 even portions and place in a cylinder-shape along the center of each pastry strip.

6. Brush 1 side of each pastry strip with egg, and tightly fold over the other side. Roll so that the pastry seam is underneath. Trim the pastry ends and slice each roll into 8. Set aside to chill on a baking sheet lined with parchment paper for 15 minutes.

7. Preheat the main oven to 390 degrees F.

8. Brush each roll lightly with egg, scatter over the sesame seeds and bake in the preheated oven for 20 minutes, until golden.

Potato, Cheese, and Marmite Pasties

These savory, meat-free hand pies are a great lite bite to munch on while on the go.

Servings: 6

Total Time: 1hour 30mins

Ingredients:

- 1 pound potatoes (peeled and grated)
- 7 ounces mature Cheddar cheese (grated)
- 3½ ounces soft breadcrumbs
- Bunch of spring onions (thinly sliced)
- 2 eggs (divided)
- Salt and black pepper (to season)
- Flour (to dust)
- 1 (17 ounces) pack shortcrust pastry
- 2 tbsp Marmite (warmed)
- Water

Directions:

1. Preheat the main oven to 320 degrees F.

2. Add the grated potato to the grated cheese, breadcrumbs, spring onions, and 1 egg to a bowl. Season with 1 teaspoon of salt and lots of black pepper. Stir well to combine.

3. On a lightly floured clean worktop, roll the pastry out to a thickness of a coin.

4. Using a 6" saucer or bowl, cut out 6 circles of shortcrust pastry, re-rolling as needed.

5. In the microwave, warm the Marmite along with a splash of water. Brush the mixture over each pastry circle leave an ⅛" border all the way around.

6. Evenly divide the filling and spoon in the center of each circle.

7. In a small bowl, beat the remaining egg, use it as a wash, and brush it around each border.

8. For each pie, bring 2 sides of pastry up to meet over the filling, and using your fingers, crimp and pinch to create a pasty shape.

9. Transfer to a baking sheet, brush all over with more egg wash and bake for 50-60 minutes, until crisp and golden.

10. Enjoy.

Savory Pancakes

Marmite is the secret ingredient to these savory pancakes to serve with creamy avocado, juicy tomatoes, and salty Greek cheese.

Servings: 4

Total Time: 20mins

Ingredients

- 2 cups self-raising flour
- 2 cups whole milk
- 2 eggs
- ¼ cup butter
- 2 tsp Marmite
- 1 avocado (peeled, pitted and sliced)
- 2 tomatoes (chopped)
- ¼ cup Greek feta cheese (crumbled)

Directions:

1. Sift the flour into a mixing bowl and create a well in the middle.

2. In a jug, whisk the milk with the eggs and add it to the flour. Whisk continually to form a smooth batter.

3. In a microwave-safe bowl, combine the butter with the Marmite and heat until the butter is melted. Cover the bowl with plastic wrap and transfer to the refrigerator for half an hour to rest.

4. Over moderate heat, heat a frying pan. Brush the pan lightly with melted butter.

5. Pour approximately ⅓ cup of the batter into the frying pan to create a 6" pancake. Cook the pancake for 2-3 minutes, until bubbles start to appear on the top and the pancake's underside is golden brown. Flip over and cook for an additional 1-2 minutes, until golden. Transfer the pancake to a plate and using a clean tea towel, cover to keep warm.

6. Repeat the process 7 more times until the batter is used up. You will need to reheat the pancakes before serving.

7. Serve the pancakes topped with sliced avocado and chopped tomatoes. Scatter with crumbled feta and enjoy.

Mains

Asian-Style Ribs

Juicy pork ribs in a sticky marinade to serve with steamed rice will tick all those taste boxes.

Servings: 4

Total Time: 35mins

Ingredients:

Pork Marinade:

- ¼ cup cornstarch
- 1 egg white
- 1 tbsp soy sauce
- 1 tsp sugar
- ½ tsp white pepper
- ½ tsp salt
- ⅛ tsp Chinese 5-spice powder

Ribs:

- 2 pound baby back rib (cut across the bones into 1" pieces)
- Canola oil
- Sesame seeds (to garnish)
- Cilantro leaves (to garnish)
- Steamed rice (to serve)

Sauce:

- 1 tsp oil (from pork)
- 1-2 tsp Marmite
- 2 tbsp runny honey
- 2 tbsp malt sugar
- 1 tbsp oyster sauce
- 1 tbsp soy sauce
- 1 tbsp hot water
- ¼ tsp garlic powder

- Dash of white pepper (to taste)
- Salt (to taste)
- Sugar (to taste)

Directions:

1. First, prepare the marinade. Add the cornstarch to the egg white, soy sauce, sugar, white pepper, salt, and Chinese 5-spice powder. Stir to combine and add the pork ribs. Set aside to marinate for 60 minutes.

2. Remove the pork from the marinade and allow to come to room temperature before cooking.

3. Add sufficient oil to a cast iron pan to fill to a ¾" depth.

4. Fry the pork, in batches for 4-5 minutes at 325 degrees F. Bring the oil to a temperature of 375 degrees F before frying the next batch of meat. Arrange the fried pork on a wire rack as you progress.

5. For the sauce, in a wok, add 1 teaspoon of cooking oil from the pork along with the Marmite, runny honey, malt sugar, oyster sauce, soy sauce, hot water, and garlic powder. Season with white pepper, salt, and sugar, to taste.

6. Set the heat to moderately high and add the pork, stirring well to coat evenly.

7. Garnish the ribs with sesame seeds, cilantro leaves, and serve with rice.

Beef, Ale, and Marmite Pie

This comforting meat pie flavored with ale and Marmite is rich and meaty. Serve with chunks of crust bread.

Servings: 4

Total Time: 4hours

Ingredients:

- 1 pound beef chuck (cubed)
- Sea salt and black pepper
- 1 tbsp vegetable oil
- 1 onion (peeled and finely chopped)
- 1 carrot (about ¾ cup)
- 1 tsp fresh thyme leaves (finely chopped)
- 1 tsp fresh rosemary leaves (finely chopped)
- 10 ounces button mushrooms (sliced)
- 1 cup ale
- 1 tbsp Marmite
- 1 cup chicken stock
- 16 ounces readymade frozen puff pastry (thawed)
- 1 egg (lightly beaten)

Directions:

1. Season the meat all over with salt and black pepper.

2. Over moderate to high heat in a Dutch oven, heat the oil.

3. Add half of the beef cubes and cook while occasionally turning, for 8 minutes or until browned all over.

4. Remove the meat from the Dutch oven and repeat the process with the remaining beef.

5. Take the beef out of the pot and add the onion along with the carrot, thyme, rosemary leaves, and mushrooms. Cook, while stirring until the mushrooms have released their juices and the onions are translucent. This step will take approximately 8 minutes.

6. Return the beef to the Dutch oven and pour in the ale, Marmite, and stock. Cover and cook for 2 hours, until tender. Season to taste and transfer to a container to cool.

7. Place an oven rack in the middle of the oven and preheat to 400 degrees F.

8. Cut the puff pastry in half and roll each portion into a ¼" thick square sufficiently large enough to drape over a 9" pie pan.

9. Transfer one half to the pie pan.

10. Spoon the now cooled beef filling into the pie shell and brush the edges lightly with beaten egg.

11. Drape the remaining half of pastry over the filling. Trim off any bits of over-hanging pastry and pinch the pastry edges to seal.

12. Make a few steam vents in the surface of the pie and brush lightly with beaten egg.

13. Bake the pie in the oven for 50-55 minutes, until golden.

14. Set the pie aside to cool before slicing.

Cheddar Cheese Cake

Spread the love and say yes to the yeast with this savory Cheddar cheesecake topped with meaty Marmite and melting cheese.

Servings: 4-8

Total Time: 55mins

Ingredients:

- 2½ ounces butter (room temperature)
- ¾ cup sugar
- Pinch of salt
- 2 eggs (beaten)
- 1½ cups self-raising flour
- 1 cup whole milk
- 2 tbsp Marmite (warmed)
- ½ cup butter (melted)
- ½ cup Cheddar cheese (freshly grated)

Directions:

1. In a bowl, cream the butter with the sugar and salt. Add the beaten eggs, and stir thoroughly to combine.

2. Sift in the flour alternating with splashes of the whole milk.

3. Transfer the mixture to a greased 8" round pie dish.

4. Bake in the oven at 355 degrees F for 40 minutes.

5. Remove the pie from the oven and spread the Marmite evenly over the surface of the hot cake.

6. Next, pour the melted butter evenly over the Marmite. Scatter the grated Cheddar over the top.

7. Return the cake to the oven for 2-3 minutes, until the Cheddar cheese is melted.

Chilli and Marmite Quarterpounders

Serve these big, juicy vegetarian-friendly burgers in soft brioche buns piled high with your favorite toppings.

Servings: 6

Total Time: 40mins

Ingredients:

- 1 (14 ounces) can white beans (drained and rinsed)
- 3 tbsp Marmite
- 1 red chili (seeded)
- 2 tbsp cashew or peanut butter
- 1 (8¾ ounces) pouch microwave pre-cooked rice
- 1 tbsp oil
- 1 small red onion (peeled and finely chopped)
- 2 cloves of garlic (peeled and finely chopped)
- 6 flat cap mushrooms (finely chopped)
- Salt and black pepper (to season)
- Flour (to dust)

Directions:

1. Preheat the main oven to 390 degrees F.

2. In a food blender, process the white beans along with the Marmite, red chili, and nut butter to a silky smooth paste. Transfer to a bowl.

3. Add the rice to the white bean mixture and with a fork, mash until combined.

4. In a frying pan, heat 1 tablespoon of oil.

5. Add the onion and garlic to the pan along with the mushrooms. Cook until the onion is softened. Season with salt and black pepper and continue cooking until the mushrooms release their liquid and it is absorbed fully. Allow the mixture to cool.

6. Once cooled, add the onion mixture to the white bean mixture and stir thoroughly to incorporate.

7. Evenly divide the mixture into 6 portions.

8. Scatter a little flour onto clean hands and shape each portion into a patty shape.

9. Lightly oil a baking tray.

10. Arrange the burgers on the tray, flipping them over once to make sure they are oiled on both sides.

11. Cook the burgers until golden brown, for 15-20 minutes.

12. Serve the burgers in a bun with toppings of choice.

Mac, Cheese 'n Marmite

Mac 'n Cheese is an iconic American dish. Next time you prepare this meal, jazz it up with Marmite.

Servings: 8-10

Total Time: 1 hour

Ingredients:

- 17 ounces small elbow macaroni
- 2¾ ounces butter
- 3 tbsp plain flour
- 2½ cups whole milk
- 1 (6 ounces) can evaporated milk
- 9 ounces strong Cheddar cheese (coarsely grated)
- Large pinch of cayenne pepper
- 1 tbsp mustard powder
- Splash of red wine vinegar
- 1 tbsp Marmite
- Salt and black pepper
- 8 ounces strong Cheddar (chopped into small chunks)
- 1¾ ounces fresh white breadcrumbs
- 1¾ ounces panko breadcrumbs
- 1¾ ounces Parmesan (grated)

Directions:

1. Preheat the main oven to 425 degrees F.

2. Cook the macaroni in a pan of boiling salted water for approximately 2 minutes less than the package directions instructions and until al dente. Drain thoroughly and toss with a knob of butter.

3. In a pan, heat the remaining butter until nut brown and frothy. Pour off 1 tablespoon into a small bowl and return the pan to the heat.

4. Scatter over the flour, whisk and cook for 3 minutes to create a sandy paste.

5. A splash at a time, add the milk. Whisk between additions and simmer until all the milk has been incorporated.

6. Next, drizzle in the evaporated milk, and a handful at a time, add the grated Cheddar cheese to form a cheesy thick sauce.

7. Stir in the cayenne pepper, mustard powder, red wine vinegar, and Marmite. Taste and season.

8. Take off the heat and stir in the pasta.

9. Stir in the chunks of Cheddar and tip the contents into a buttered casserole dish.

10. In a bowl, combine the breadcrumbs with the Parmesan. Season with a pinch each of cayenne and sea salt.

11. Sprinkle the crumbs over the macaroni and drizzle with the brown butter, set aside earlier.

12. Bake in the oven for 30-35 minutes until crunchy and bubbling.

13. Set aside to stand for 10 minutes before enjoying.

Marmite-Butter Roast Chicken

A simple roast chicken is the perfect mid-week meal, but this doesn't mean you can't give your bird a little bit of oomph.

Servings: 6

Total Time: 1hour 20mins

Ingredients:

- 3 tbsp unsalted butter
- 1 tbsp Marmite
- ½ tsp freshly ground black pepper
- 1 (4 pounds) chicken

Directions:

1. Preheat the main oven to 400 degrees F.

2. In a 10" skillet, melt the butter over moderate heat.

3. Whisk in the Marmite and black pepper, until incorporated.

4. Transfer the Marmite butter into a container.

5. Truss the chicken and add it to the skillet. Brush it all over with half of the butter mixture.

6. Transfer the chicken to the preheated oven and roast for 45 minutes.

7. Brush the chicken with the remaining Marmite butter and continue roasting for half an hour, until the meat registers 165 degrees F.

8. Allow the chicken to rest for 15 minutes before serving.

Marmite Pad Thai

This British cupboard staple adds a new twist to this Thai dish. It makes the perfect weekend treat and is a lot healthier than the take-out version.

Servings: 4-6

Total Time: 35mins

Ingredients:

- 1 cup hot water (divided)
- 1 tbsp Marmite
- 1 tbsp fish sauce
- 1 tbsp soy sauce
- 1 tbsp brown sugar
- 8 ounces pad Thai rice noodles
- 3 tbsp vegetable oil
- 4 scallions (sliced)
- 1 shallot (sliced)
- 1 garlic clove (peeled and sliced)
- 8 ounces bean sprouts
- 5 ounces snow peas (sliced)
- 2 large eggs (beaten)
- Roasted peanuts (to garnish)
- Cilantro (chopped, to garnish)
- Sriracha sauce (to serve)
- Wedges of fresh lime (to serve)

Directions:

1. Combine ¾ cup of hot water with Marmite, fish sauce, soy sauce, and brown sugar until incorporated. Set aside.

2. Soak the noodles in hot water, set aside for 10 minutes before draining.

3. In a wok or frying pan, heat the oil over high heat.

4. When the oil is sizzling hot, add the scallions followed by the shallot and garlic, stirring well for 5-6 minutes until browned.

5. Stir in the bean sprouts along with the snow peas and cook, while stirring for approximately 4 minutes, until crisp yet tender.

6. Whisk the eggs into the veggie mixture in the pan and cook while whisking until the eggs are sufficiently cooked.

7. Add the sauce and noodles set aside earlier and cook while stirring until the noodles have absorbed the liquid.

8. Garnish with roasted peanuts and chopped cilantro. Drizzle with Sriracha sauce and serve with wedges of fresh lime.

Peanut Butter and Marmite Marinated Baked Tempeh

Move over meat! Marmite will add flavor to this veggie tempeh in a rich and creamy marinade.

Servings: 2

Total Time: 8hours 20mins

Ingredients:

- 2 tsp smoked olive oil
- 1 tsp smooth peanut butter
- ½ tsp Marmite
- 1 tsp store-bought BBQ sauce
- 1 tsp soy sauce
- 7 ounces tempeh (sliced)

Directions:

1. In a mixing bowl, combine the olive oil with the peanut butter, Marmite, BBQ sauce, and soy sauce.

2. Add the tempeh to the bowl and mix to coat evenly. Cover the bowl with plastic wrap and transfer it to the fridge overnight.

3. Preheat the main oven to 355 degrees F.

4. Using parchment paper, line a baking tray.

5. Remove the tempeh from the marinade, shaking off any excess.

6. Arrange the tempeh on the baking tray and bake on the middle rack of the preheated oven until golden, for approximately 15 minutes.

Spaghetti Marmite Carbonara

Mama Mia! Not sure what nonna would say to add Marmite to this Italian pasta dish, but it does add depth and flavor.

Servings: 2

Total Time: 15mins

Ingredients:

- 2 egg yolks
- 2 tsp Marmite
- 1 ounce Parmesan cheese (grated)
- Freshly ground black pepper
- 6 ounces spaghetti
- 1 large garlic clove (peeled and squashed)
- 4½ ounces pancetta (diced)
- Extra-virgin olive oil
- Parmesan (grated, to serve)
- Fresh parsley (finely chopped, to garnish)

Directions:

1. Bring a large saucepan of salted water to boil.

2. In a bowl, mash the egg yolks with the Marmite and grated cheese. Season with freshly ground black pepper.

3. When the water comes to boil, add the spaghetti and cook until al dente.

4. In a cold frying pan, combine the garlic with the pancetta in 2 tablespoons of olive oil. Bring to moderate heat and fry until the garlic is crisp and golden. Remove and discard the garlic.

5. Drain the pasta and set a small cup of pasta cooking liquid to one side.

6. Remove the frying pan from the heat.

7. Add the drained pasta to the pan, followed by the Marmite mixture, and pour in a splash of the pasta cooking liquid.

8. Toss to combine and coat evenly and serve garnished with more grated cheese and chopped parsley.

Spicy Marmite Salmon

Spice up seafood with sweet chili sauce and rich and flavorful Marmite. It's ready from pan to plate in less than half an hour.

Servings: 4

Total Time: 25mins

Ingredients:

- 1 tbsp Marmite
- 2 tsp hot water
- 1 tbsp sweet chili sauce
- 1¼ pounds salmon fillet (skin removed, rinsed and patted dry)
- ¼ tsp salt
- ¼ tsp ground black pepper
- 1 tsp vegetable oil

Directions:

1. Using parchment paper, line a baking tray.

2. In a bowl, combine the Marmite with the hot water and chili sauce.

3. Season the salmon with salt and black pepper.

4. Drizzle the Marmite mixture over the salmon and set aside for 10 minutes.

5. Grill the salmon for approximately 6 minutes.

6. Take the salmon out from the grill, and with a spoon, scoop the sauce mixture from the sides of the baking tray and baste the salmon.

7. Drizzle the fish with oil and return to the grill for an additional 4-6 minutes. The internal temperature of the salmon should be 145 degrees F.

8. Serve and enjoy.

Sides Snacks

Charred Brussels Sprouts with Marmite Butter

Here, we combine two main ingredients that you will either love or hate. If you are a fan of both, then this side dish is the one for you.

Servings: 4

Total Time: 15mins

Ingredients:

- 3½ ounces unsalted butter (softened)
- 3 tsp Marmite
- 17½ ounces Brussels sprouts (cleaned and halved)
- Salt and black pepper (to season)

Directions:

1. In a bowl, beat the butter with the Marmite until silky smooth.

2. Form the mixture into a log shape on a sheet of parchment paper. Roll and twist the end of the paper to resemble a Christmas cracker. Transfer to the fridge to chill until ready to use.

3. In a pan, boil the Brussels sprouts for 3-4 minutes. Drain and set aside to steam dry.

4. Heat a frying pan. Add the Brussels sprouts to the pan and dry-fry for 4-5 minutes, until they begin to blacken on their cut sides and edges.

5. Remove the frying pan from the heat.

6. Add the Marmite butter and allow the butter to sizzle and melt while shaking the pan to coat the sprouts. Use as much Marmite butter for preferred level of taste. Store any leftover butter in the fridge for up to 7 days.

7. Season to taste with salt and pepper and serve.

Greek-Style Stuffed Tomatoes with Marmite and Pine Nuts

You don't need a holiday to enjoy a taste of Greece when you can enjoy these juicy, delicious stuffed tomatoes. Serve as a side or snack.

Servings: 4-6

Total Time: 1hour 10mins

Ingredients:

- 8-10 large ripe tomatoes
- 8¾ ounces risotto
- 1 ounce wild rice
- 3 ounces garden peas
- 1 medium zucchini (shredded)
- Extra-virgin olive oil
- 2 tbsp parsley (finely chopped)
- 1 clove garlic (peeled and minced)
- Pinch of turmeric
- Pinch of oregano
- Pine nuts (finely chopped)
- Marmite (to taste)
- Greek feta (crumbled, to garnish)

Directions:

1. First, prepare the tomatoes by chopping off their tops. Using a spoon, scoop out the insides of the tomatoes, transferring them to a bowl. Discard the core.

2. Place the tomatoes along with their tops (lids) upside down in a glass casserole dish and allow them to drain.

3. Cook the risotto and wild rice for 20 minutes and combine.

4. Combine the risotto and rice with the peas and zucchini, juice from the tomatoes, a splash of olive oil, parsley, garlic, and a pinch each of turmeric and oregano.

5. Finally, fold in the pine nuts along with the Marmite. The amount of Marmite will depend on your personal preference.

6. Stir the filling well to combine and spoon it into the empty tomato shells.

7. Preheat the oven to 350 degrees F.

8. Arrange the filled tomatoes on a baking tray, drizzle with lots of olive oil and bake in the oven for 35-40 minutes, until the tomatoes are on the point of collapse.

9. Sprinkle crumbled feta over the stuffed tomatoes and serve.

Marmite Cheesy Straws

Buttery melt-in-the-mouth cheesy straws are the perfect nibble or snack to serve with wine, beer, or soda.

Servings: 20

Total Time: 35mins

Ingredients:

- Plain flour (to dust)
- 1 (11 ounces) sheet all-butter puff pastry
- 1½ tbsp Marmite
- 3 ounces strong Cheddar cheese (finely grated, divided)
- 1 egg yolk (beaten)

Directions:

1. Using parchment paper line 2 baking sheets.

2. Liberally flour a clean work surface.

3. Unroll the pastry onto the work surface with the shortest edge closest to you.

4. Spread the Marmite evenly over the top half.

5. Scatter 2 ounces of cheese on top of the Marmite.

6. Fold the lower half of the pastry over to enclose the filling.

7. Re-roll the filled pastry to a 14x7" rectangle of approximately ⅛" thick.

8. Brush the pastry lightly with egg yolk and scatter over the remaining cheese. Slice widthwise into ¾" strips. Twist each strip gently into a spiral and arrange the spirals on the prepared baking sheets.

9. Preheat the main oven to 390 degrees F. and cook until golden, for 15-20 minutes.

10. Transfer the straws to a wire baking rack and serve warm.

Marmite Glazed Nuts and Seeds

This combination of nuts and seeds and flavored with sweet sugar and salty Marmite is a healthy alternative to any store-bought snack.

Servings: 8

Total Time: 25mins

Ingredients:

- 1 egg white
- 2 tbsp Marmite
- 2 tbsp light brown sugar
- 2½ ounces whole almonds
- 2½ ounces cashew nuts
- 1¾ ounces pecan nuts
- 2½ ounces pumpkin seeds
- ¾ ounces sunflower seeds
- 2 tbsp sesame seeds
- 1 tsp ground coriander
- ½ tsp ground cayenne pepper
- ¼ tsp chili flakes

Directions:

1. Preheat the main oven to 400 degrees F.

2. In a bowl, combine the egg white with the Marmite. Add the sugar, stir to incorporate.

3. Add the almonds, cashews, pecans, pumpkin seeds, sunflower seeds, and sesame seeds to a large bowl. Add the egg white mixture to the nuts and seeds and toss to evenly coat.

4. Spread the mixture evenly on 1-2 baking sheets and place in the preheated oven for 10 minutes.

5. Scatter over the coriander, cayenne pepper, and chili flakes. Mix well and return to the oven for an additional 5 minutes. The mixture is ready when it is golden, toasted, and sticky. If after 5 minutes it isn't, then continue roasting for another 4-5 minutes.

6. Remove from the oven and allow to cool on the baking sheets, stirring occasionally.

7. Store the cooled nuts in an airtight resealable container for up to 14 days.

Marmite Hummus

Give regular hummus a salty twist with marvelous Marmite.

Servings: 4

Total Time: 5mins

Ingredients:

- 1 (14 ounces) can garbanzo beans (drained, and rinsed)
- 1 tsp garlic and herb salt
- 1 tsp ground cumin
- 1 cup filtered water
- 1 tsp Marmite
- Freshly squeezed juice of 1 lemon
- ½ cup tahini

Directions:

1. Add the garbanzo beans, garlic and herb salt, cumin, filtered water, Marmite and fresh lemon juice to a food blender, and process to a smooth paste.

2. Add the tahini followed by additional water, if needed to achieve your preferred consistency.

3. Serve with veggie batons or pita.

Marmite Popcorn

Recreate the comforting taste of buttery toast and Marmite with this pop-in-the-mouth snack.

Servings: 4

Total Time: 20mins

Ingredients:

- 1-2 tbsp sunflower oil
- 2 ounces popping corn
- 1¾ tbsp butter
- 2 tsp Marmite
- Cheese (grated, to serve)

Directions:

1. Preheat the main oven to 300 degrees F. Using greaseproof paper cover a baking tray.

2. Pour the sunflower oil into a large saucepan over moderate to high heat.

3. When the oil is hot, add the popping corn and gently shake the pan, so the popcorn kernels are in one layer and coated evenly in the oil.

4. Cover the pan with a lid and leave on the heat while gently shaking every 30 seconds. The popcorn is ready when the pops are 2-3 seconds apart. Tip the popcorn into a bowl.

5. Over low heat, in a small saucepan, melt the butter and stir in the Marmite to create a glossy, smooth liquid.

6. Pour the Marmite mixture over the popped corn and stir thoroughly until each piece is coated evenly.

7. Spread the popcorn evenly over the parchment-lined baking tray and transfer to the oven for 3-4 minutes, to crisp.

8. Scatter the grated cheese over the popcorn and enjoy.

Onion and Marmite Fritters

Reinvent the onion bhaji with this ultimate bar snack. These crisp veggie fritters are easy to make and 100 percent moreish.

Servings: 4

Total Time: 30mins

Ingredients:

- 3 eggs (beaten)
- ¼ cup milk
- 2 tsp Marmite
- ½ tsp fresh thyme (finely chopped)
- ½ cup + 1 tbsp all-purpose flour
- ¼ tsp baking powder
- Sea salt and freshly ground black pepper
- 4 cups sliced sweet onion (sliced)
- 1 quart peanut oil
- 2 tbsp fresh parsley leaves (chopped)

Directions:

1. In a bowl, whisk the eggs with the milk, Marmite, and thyme until combined.

2. In a second bowl, whisk the flour with the baking powder. Add a pinch of sea salt and a dash of black pepper.

3. Whisk the dry ingredients into the wet ingredients,

4. Toss in the onions, and using a spatula, gently crush the slices of onion. Set aside to rest for half an hour.

5. Preheat the main oven to 300 degrees F. Place an aluminum foil-lined baking sheet in the preheated oven.

6. In a large pan over moderate heat, heat 3" of oil until it reaches 325 degrees F. If you don't have a thermometer, you can test the heat by dropping in a slice of onion. If the onion sizzles, the oil is sufficiently hot.

7. Carefully drop in ¼ cup size fritters into the hot oil. Cook while frequently turning until they are golden, for approximately 4 minutes.

8. Transfer the fritters to a baking rack set in a baking tray and place the now cooked fritters into the oven to keep warm while you prepare the remaining fritters.

9. Serve the fritters garnished with parsley.

Roast Potatoes with Marmite

Who doesn't love a good roastie? But next time you roast potatoes, add a spoonful of Marmite to add color and flavor.

Servings: 4

Total Time: 40mins

Ingredients:

- 4 large potatoes (peeled, quartered, and rinsed in cold water)
- Boiling water
- 1 tbsp Marmite
- Nonstick cooking spray

Directions:

1. Add the potatoes to a large pan. Pour in boiling water and bring to boil over moderate to high heat. Simmer for 10 minutes, or until the potatoes are beginning to soften.

2. Pour the potatoes into a colander and shake well to fluff the potatoes up.

3. Preheat the main oven to 355 degrees F.

4. Add the potatoes to a deep-sided casserole dish.

5. Add the Marmite and mix gently to coat while trying not to break them up.

6. Spritz the potatoes with nonstick spray and bake in the oven for 35-40 minutes, until the potatoes are crisp on the outside and fluffy on the inside.

7. Enjoy.

Roasted Cauliflower with Camembert and Marmite

If you are planning a special family meal, then this ooey-gooey, savory side dish is a game-changer.

Servings: 4-6

Total Time: 1hour 30mins

Ingredients:

- 1 whole cauliflower (leaves removed)
- 1 clove garlic (peeled and halved)
- 3 sprigs rosemary
- Salt and black pepper
- Olive oil
- 2 tbsp Marmite
- 1 ounce butter (melted)
- 1¼ cups double cream
- 1¾ ounces Parmesan (grated)
- ¾ cup vegetable stock
- Whole nutmeg (to grate)
- 8¾ ounces Camembert

Directions:

1. Preheat the main oven to 355 degrees F.

2. Trim the stalk for the cauliflower and sit the cauliflower upright in a large ovenproof dish.

3. Rub the cut sides of the garlic along with the rosemary sprigs and season liberally with salt and black pepper.

4. Add the sprigs of rosemary to the pan along with the cauliflower, drizzle with oil and place in the oven for approximately 45 minutes, to roast.

5. In the meantime, combine the Marmite with the melted butter and set aside.

6. In a pan, heat the double cream along with the grated Parmesan and stock. Crush in the clove of garlic.

7. Grate in approximately ¼ of the whole nutmeg and allow to simmer for 5 minutes—season with a pinch of salt and a dash of black pepper.

8. When 45 minutes have elapsed, brush the Marmite and butter all over the cauliflower.

9. Carefully, using a sharp knife. Cut out the top section of the cauliflower. Add the unwrapped Camembert to the space and score it all over.

10. Pour the creamy sauce into the dish and cook for an additional 10-15 minutes, until the sauce bubbles, and the cheese oozes. The cauliflower should be caramelized.

11. Serve and enjoy.

Wholemeal Marmite Bread

Add a kick to mealtimes with marvelous Marmite. It gives a rich, molasses flavor to wholemeal, homemade bread.

Servings: 1 loaf

Total Time: 1hour 30mins

Ingredients:

- 17 ounces strong wholemeal bread flour
- 1½ ounces molasses
- 2 tsp fine salt
- 1¼ cups warm water (divided)
- 1 (¼ ounce) sachet fast-action yeast
- 2 tbsp Marmite
- Knob of butter (melted, to grease)
- Flour (to dust)

Directions:

1. Using an electric mixer fitted with a dough hook, combine the flour with the molasses and salt.

2. Measure out the warm water and in a second bowl, add a quarter of the water to the yeast to dissolve, and create a cloudy liquid.

3. Add the yeast to the flour mixture.

4. Turn the mixer to its lowest speed setting and begin to add the remaining water to the mixture and beat slowly until it forms a dough.

5. Add the Marmite and beat on moderate speed for 12 minutes.

6. When 12 minutes have elapsed, remove the dough from the mixer and knead by hand for 5 minutes on a lightly floured work surface.

7. Transfer to a clean bowl, cover with a clean damp tea towel and set aside in the fridge overnight to prove.

8. Once proven, remove from the bowl and return to the food mixer fitted with a dough hook. Begin to knock back the dough on moderate speed for 10 minutes before removing from the electric mixer. Remove from the mixer.

9. Line a loaf pan with melted butter and dust lightly with flour.

10. Shape the dough into a sausage shape and place it in the loaf pan.

11. Prove the dough while covered with a damp tea towel for 6 hours, until doubled in size.

12. Bake in the oven at 400 degrees F for 45 minutes.

13. Serve warm or toasted with lashings of butter.

Desserts Sweet Treats

Chocolate Fudge Caramels with Marmite

A chewy chocolate fudge sits on top of a rich Marmite salted caramel. The result is a unique sweet and salty candy that all of your adventurous Marmite-loving friends and family will enjoy.

Servings: 18

Total Time: 35mins

Ingredients:

Fudge:

- 10½ ounces dark chocolate squares
- 10½ ounces condensed milk

Caramel:

- 1 tbsp golden syrup
- 3½ ounces condensed milk
- 2 tbsp golden caster sugar
- 2 tsp Marmite
- 2 tbsp butter

Directions:

1. Line a large square baking tin with parchment paper.

2. First, prepare the fudge. Using a double boiler, melt together the dark chocolate and condensed milk. Pour the mixture into the prepared baking tin and chill for 30-60 minutes until firm.

3. Next, prepare the caramel. Add all of the ingredients (golden syrup, condensed milk, golden caster sugar, Marmite, and butter) to a small saucepan and place over moderate heat. Bring the mixture to a boil, continually stirring.

4. Turn the heat down to a low simmer and cook for 5 minutes, still stirring. The mixture should be chewy and soft. Take off the heat and allow to cool for 5 minutes.

5. Using a spatula, spoon the Marmite caramel over the chocolate fudge in an even layer. Chill for another 30-60 minutes until set.

6. When the fudge caramels are set, take out of the refrigerator and slice into squares using a knife dipped in boiling water, this will make the cutting easier.

Dark Chocolate Marmite Coated Potato Chips

A truly unique snack that is surprisingly addictive. If you love salty-sweet combos, then you will go crazy for these crunchy potato chips enrobed in Marmite-salted dark chocolate.

Servings: 3-4

Total Time: 25mins

Ingredients:

- 1 tsp Marmite
- 3½ ounces good-quality dark chocolate
- 1¾ ounces ridged salted potato chips

Directions:

1. Cover a baking sheet with parchment paper.

2. Using a double boiler set up, melt together the Marmite and dark chocolate, stirring gently. Take off the heat.

3. One at a time, dip the salted potato chips into the melted chocolate to coat, then place on the baking sheet.

4. Chill the potato chips until the chocolate coating has set. Enjoy!

Macarons with Marmite Ganache Filling

Believe it or not, history suggests that the macaron cookie is actually Italian in origin, not French, as most people assume. These sweet treats were first brought to France in 1533 by a Florentine noblewoman, Catherine di Medici, for her wedding to future King of France, Henry II. These crisp little cookies are still popular today. This particular version, with a bittersweet Marmite ganache filling, is bound to get your tastebuds tingling.

Servings: 36

Total Time: 3hours 30mins*

Ingredients:

Ganache Filling:

- 1 cup water
- 1¾ ounces Marmite
- 1¼ cups brown sugar
- 13 ounces 65% cocoa dark chocolate (chopped)

Macaron Cookies:

- 1⅓ cups confectioner's sugar
- 10 tsp water
- Whites of 3 eggs
- 2 tbsp cocoa powder
- 6½ ounces ground almonds
- ¾ cup + 1 tbsp granulated sugar

Directions:

1. First, prepare the ganache. Bring the water, Marmite, and brown sugar to a boil in a saucepan over high heat, turn down to a simmer and cook for 5 minutes.

2. Add the chopped chocolate to a bowl and pour over the hot Marmite mixture. Stir until the chocolate has melted. You may need to use a stick blender if the chocolate does not melt easily. Allow the mixture to cool and then transfer it to the refrigerator for 1 day.

3. The following day, prepare the macaron cookies—Preheat the main oven to 340 degrees F and line 4 cookie sheets with parchment paper.

4. Add the confectioner's sugar and water to a saucepan over moderate heat, stir until the sugar dissolves. Bring the mixture to a boil until it reaches 245 degrees F.

5. Using an electric mixer, whisk half of the egg whites until frothy.

6. With the mixer still running, slowly pour in the hot sugar mixture and continue to whisk until the mixture can hold stiff peaks; this will take approximately 5 minutes.

7. In the meantime, add the cocoa powder, ground almonds, and granulated sugar to a food processor and blitz to a fine powder. Sift the mixture into a mixing bowl and beat in the remaining egg whites until paste-like.

8. Fold the almond paste into the stiff egg white mixture until incorporated.

9. Transfer the mixture to a piping bag and pipe, 72 evenly-sized rounds onto the cookie sheets.

10. Tap the cookie sheets against the worktop to burst any small air bubbles from the macarons. Bake each tray of cookies in the oven for 12 minutes, turn the tray halfway through cooking.

11. Allow the macarons to cool completely before removing them from the cookie sheets.

12. Sandwich equally-sized cookies together using the prepared Marmite Grenache to create 36 macarons.

13. Transfer the finished macarons to an airtight container and allow to rest for 1-2 hours before serving.

*Plus 1-day chilling time for the ganache.

Marmite Dulce de Leche Cake

Rich, salty Marmite is the perfect partner to sweet and creamy Dulche de Leche. This ooey-gooey cake with fluffy buttercream frosting will be a hit with adventurous kids and grownups alike.

Servings: 16

Total Time: 1hour 15mins

Ingredients:

Sponge:

- 4 tbsp dulce de leche
- ¾ cup butter
- ¾ cup light muscovado sugar
- 1½ cups self-raising flour
- ½ tsp baking powder
- 2 tbsp ground almonds
- 3 eggs

Frosting:

- ⅔ cup butter
- 7 ounces golden confectioner's sugar
- 4 tbsp dulce de leche
- 1 tsp Marmite

Directions:

1. Preheat the main oven to 225 degrees F. Line a 9" square baking tin with parchment paper.

2. First, prepare the sponge. Pour the dulce de leche into the base of the baking tin and smooth in an even layer using a silicone spatula.

3. Add the butter and sugar to an electric mixer and beat until creamy.

4. Sift the baking powder, flour, and almonds together into a bowl. With the mixer running, add the dry ingredients to the mixer bowl in three batches, adding an egg between each addition. When the mixture is smooth and combined, pour it into the prepared cake tin.

5. Place in the oven and bake for 30 minutes until set in the center.

6. Take the cake out of the oven and allow to cool for 5-10 minutes before inverting the baked cake onto a wire rack and remove the piece of parchment paper. Scrape any dulce de leche stuck to the paper and smear it back onto the top of the cake.

7. Next, prepare the frosting. Using an electric mixer, beat the butter until creamy and soft. Add half of the confectioner's sugar and beat until incorporated. Add the dulce de leche, Marmite, and the remaining confectioner's sugar and continue to beat until fluffy and combined. If the frosting is too thick, add a drop of milk.

8. Spread the frosting over the top of the cooled cake and slice into squares. Enjoy!

Millionaire's Marmite Shortbread

Elevate already decadent Millionaire's Shortbread to a whole new level with the addition of Marmite and enjoy the perfect combination of sweet and salty flavors with every bite.

Servings: 20

Total Time: 1hour 15mins

Ingredients:

Marmite Caramel:

- 8¾ ounces granulated sugar
- 1⅓ cups heavy cream
- 1¾ ounces unsalted butter
- 2 tsp Marmite

Shortbread:

- ¾ cup unsalted butter (chilled, chopped)
- 1¾ cups plain flour
- ⅓ cup superfine sugar

Chocolate Topping:

- 12¼ ounces dark chocolate
- 12¼ ounces white chocolate

Directions:

1. First, make the caramel. Add the sugar to a large saucepan and place over low heat and do not stir. As the sugar begins to melt at the perimeter, use a spatula to push large piles of sugar towards the melting edges so that it melts evenly.

2. Continue to heat the sugar until it turns a rich amber color, before it burns, take the caramel off the heat quickly.

3. Stirring the caramel vigorously, pour in half of the cream. The mixture may bubble, so take care.

4. Return the caramel to the heat while continuing to stir, until any clumps melt.

5. Add the butter, Marmite, and remaining cream and stir to combine. Continue to heat for 2-3 more minutes until the mixture thickens to a caramel-like texture.

6. Take the caramel off the heat and pour it into a bowl. Set aside to cool.

7. Next, prepare the shortbread—Preheat the main oven to 300 degrees F. Line a 10" square baking tin with parchment paper.

8. Add the butter and flour to a food processor and pulse to a breadcrumb-like texture. Add the sugar and pulse again to combine.

9. Tip the shortbread mixture into the base of the prepare baking tin and press it into an even, compact layer. Place in the oven and bake for 30 minutes until golden. Take out of the oven and allow to cool completely.

10. Pour the cooled caramel over the cooled shortbread layer, chill until the caramel layer has set.

11. For the topping, melt the dark chocolate using a double boiler set up. Take off the heat and allow to cool a little before pouring over the caramel layer. Use a palette knife to spread the dark chocolate out evenly.

12. Add the white chocolate to a microwave-safe bowl and melt in the microwave in short 5-10 second intervals. Drizzle the white chocolate over the dark chocolate layer in an attractive pattern.

13. Return to the refrigerator until set completely before slicing and serving.

Mocha Marmite Cake

Dark chocolate, coffee, and Marmite combine in this devilishly dark triple-layered sponge cake. Enjoy with a cup of hot, freshly-brewed coffee.

Servings: 16

Total Time: 1hour 15mins

Ingredients:

- Butter (to grease)

Sponge:

- 1 cup unsalted butter
- 1 cup black coffee (cooled)
- 2¼ ounces cocoa powder
- 5¼ ounces dark chocolate (chopped)
- 1¾ cups brown sugar
- 1 tbsp vanilla essence
- 4 eggs
- Yolks of 2 eggs
- 1½ cups plain flour
- 2¼ tsp baking powder
- ½ tsp salt

Frosting:

- ½ cup butter
- ¾ cup whole milk
- 2¼ cups brown sugar
- 2 tbsp Marmite
- 4 cups confectioner's sugar
- Dark chocolate curls (to decorate)

Directions:

1. Preheat the main oven to 355 degrees F and grease three 7" cake tins with butter then line with parchment paper.

2. Using a double boiler, gently melt together the butter and black coffee, stirring often. Take off the heat and stir in the cocoa powder and chopped dark chocolate. Continue to stir until the dark chocolate has melted.

3. Next, stir in the brown sugar and vanilla essence until combined. Then whisk in the whole eggs and egg yolks.

4. Finally, sift the flour, baking powder, and salt together into a bowl. Fold the dry ingredients into the chocolate mixture until incorporated.

5. Pour the cake batter evenly into the 3 prepared cake tins. Place in the oven and bake for 30-35 minutes until set in the center.

6. Take the cakes out of the oven and allow to cool completely.

7. When the cake has cooled, prepare the frosting. In a saucepan over low heat, melt the butter. Add the milk, brown sugar, and Marmite, stir and heat until the mixture begins to bubble and boil, after 60 seconds pour the mixture into a bowl along with half of the confectioner's sugar and whisk to combine.

8. Set aside the mixture to cool completely, whisk at intervals during the cooling process.

9. When the frosting is cool, whisk in the remaining confectioner's sugar.

10. Stack the three cooled sponges on top of each other, spreading a ¼ of the frosting between each sponge layer. Cover the outside of the cake evenly with the remaining frosting.

11. Decorate the top of the cake with the dark chocolate shavings, slice, and enjoy!

Peanut Butter and Marmite Rolls

These peanut butter and Marmite rolls are like the cinnamon rolls, more fun, and adventurous relative! With warm spices and a sticky peanut butter-Marmite filling, you'll definitely want to go back for seconds!

Servings: 36

Total Time: 3hours 30mins*

Ingredients:

Rolls:

- 1 tbsp ground flaxseeds
- 3 tbsp water
- 2¼ tsp dry active yeast
- ⅓ cup granulated sugar
- ¾ cup almond milk (warmed)
- ¼ cup coconut oil
- 1 tsp vanilla essence
- 3 cups all-purpose flour
- 1 tsp ground cardamom
- ½ tsp ground nutmeg
- 1 tsp sea salt
- Olive oil (to grease)

Filling:

- 1 tsp Marmite
- ⅔ cup peanut butter
- 1 tbsp butter

Directions:

1. Add the flaxseeds and water to a small bowl and stir to combine. Set aside for 5 minutes to thicken.

2. Stir the yeast and 1 tbsp sugar into the warm milk until combined; allow to soak for 5-10 minutes.

3. Next, stir the coconut oil, vanilla essence, and flaxseed mixture into the almond milk/yeast.

4. In a clean bowl, combine the flour, cardamom, nutmeg, salt, and remaining sugar. Make a well in the center of the dry ingredients and pour in the wet ingredients. Mix the dough using a wooden spoon until wet. Continue to mix the dough with clean hands until it begins to come together.

5. At this point, tip the dough out onto a floured worktop and continue to knead until smooth, elastic, and well combined. Shape the dough into a large ball and transfer to a bowl greased with olive oil.

6. Cover the bowl with plastic wrap and set in a warm place for an hour to double in size.

7. In the meantime, prepare the filling. Combine the Marmite, peanut butter, and butter in a small bowl using a whisk.

8. Tip the risen dough back out onto a floured worktop and roll into a rectangular sheet a ¼" thick. Smear the filling mixture over the top of the dough.

9. Roll the dough sheet up tightly, starting at the widest side, then slice the roll into 8-10 equal pieces.

10. Line a baking sheet with parchment paper.

11. Arrange the rolls on the prepared baking sheet, a few inches apart from one another, and cover the baking sheet loosely with a kitchen towel. Set in a warm place for 40 minutes to rise.

12. Preheat the main oven to 350 degrees F.

13. Place the rolls in the oven and bake for 15-20 minutes until golden. Allow to cool a little before serving.

Pistachio and Marmite Truffle Squares

Serve these unique and decadent pistachio Marmite truffles at your next get together. They're guaranteed to be a conversation starter!

Servings: 36

Total Time: 3hours 25mins

Ingredients:

- Canola oil (to grease)
- 7 ounces plain chocolate (broken into smaller pieces)
- 3½ ounces 70% cocoa dark chocolate (broken into smaller pieces)
- 1¼ cups heavy cream
- 1 tsp instant coffee granules
- 1 tbsp Marmite
- 3½ ounces shelled pistachios (chopped finely)

Directions:

1. Grease an 8" square baking tin with canola oil and line with plastic kitchen wrap.

2. Using a double boiler set up, gently melt together the chocolates, cream, coffee granules, and Marmite, while stirring often.

3. Take off the heat and pour into the prepared baking tin. Allow to cool to room temperature, then sprinkle over the chopped pistachios. Transfer the mixture to the refrigerator for 3 hours until set.

4. Gently lift the set slab out of the baking tin and slice into 36 squares. Keep chilled until ready serve.

Polenta Poke Cake with Marmite Butter

Holes are poked into a soft and fluffy polenta cake; then, a melted Marmite butter is poured over, soaking into the sponge and resulting in the most moist and delicious cake you've ever tasted!

Servings: 3-4

Total Time: 25mins

Ingredients:

Cake:

- ⅓ cup butter
- ¾ cup granulated sugar
- Pinch salt
- 1 egg
- 1½ cups self-raising flour
- 1 cup whole milk
- 1 tbsp polenta

Marmite Butter:

- ½ cup butter
- 2 tsp Marmite

Directions:

1. Preheat the main oven to 375 degrees F.

2. Using an electric mixer, beat together the butter and sugar until creamy.

3. Add the salt and egg and continue to mix until combined.

4. Sift the flour into the mixer in batches, alternating with splashes of whole milk until both are incorporated.

5. Transfer the batter to an 8" square baking tin.

6. Sprinkle over the polenta, then place in the oven and bake for 35-40 minutes.

7. Take the cake out of the oven.

8. Immediately after, melt together the butter and Marmite in a small saucepan, stir until combined.

9. Poke holes in the top of the just-baked cake and pour over the Marmite butter. Allow to cool a little more before slicing and serving.

Sweet 'n Salty Popsicles

Love 'em or hate 'em, these icy popsicles are a real talking point.

Servings: 8

Total Time: 40mins

Ingredients:

- ⅔ cup caster sugar
- ½ cup cocoa
- ¼ cup runny honey
- 2 tbsp Marmite
- 3 tsp cornflour
- 1 tsp vanilla essence
- 1 cup whole milk
- 1 cup thickened cream (whipped)

Directions:

1. In a pan, combine the sugar with the cocoa, honey, Marmite, cornflour, vanilla essence, and whole milk.

2. Whisk the mixture over moderate heat until smooth. Bring to boil before reducing the heat and simmering gently until a custard-like consistency.

3. Remove the pan from the heat and pour into a heatproof bowl. Chill.

4. Fold the cream through the mixture and pour into an 8-hole popsicle mold.

5. Transfer to the freezer until solid.

Author's Afterthoughts

I would like to express my deepest thanks to you, the reader, for making this investment in one my books. I cherish the thought of bringing the love of cooking into your home.

With so much choice out there, I am grateful you decided to Purch this book and read it from beginning to end.

Please let me know by submitting an Amazon review if you enjoyed this book and found it contained valuable information to help you in your culinary endeavors. Please take a few minutes to express your opinion freely and honestly. This will help others make an informed decision on purchasing and provide me with valuable feedback.

Thank you for taking the time to review!

Christina Tosch

About the Author

Christina Tosch is a successful chef and renowned cookbook author from Long Grove, Illinois. She majored in Liberal Arts at Trinity International University and decided to pursue her passion of cooking when she applied to the world renowned Le Cordon Bleu culinary school in Paris, France. The school was lucky to recognize the immense talent of this chef and she excelled in her courses, particularly Haute Cuisine. This skill was recognized and rewarded by several highly regarded Chicago restaurants, where she was offered the prestigious position of head chef.

Christina and her family live in a spacious home in the Chicago area and she loves to grow her own vegetables and herbs in the garden she lovingly cultivates on her sprawling estate. Her and her husband have two beautiful children, 3 cats, 2 dogs and a parakeet they call Jasper. When Christina is not hard at work creating beautiful meals for Chicago's elite, she is hard at work writing engaging e-books of which she has sold over 1500.

Make sure to keep an eye out for her latest books that offer helpful tips, clear instructions and witty anecdotes that will bring a smile to your face as you read!

Printed in Great Britain
by Amazon